Masks & Mirrors

Perceptions Conceptions Projections

John P. Hinton

Masks & Mirrors
Perceptions Conceptions Projections

John P. Hinton

To my beautiful wife Debra
muse, best friend, and lover

C O N T E N T S

P R E F A C E

Masks & Mirrors is a result of inner graphic and poetic inquiry over a period of months in 2009. The colored pencil renderings are pixels of imperfect inner process birthed and brought forth with the intention of displaying creative conundrums and dubious deliberations.

The pictures are raw, unschooled, unrefined, and at times sublime renderings of emptying mediations & meditations.

The intention behind the pictures is not to reveal fine art and artistic mastery, but rather the unrefined renderings of soul discovering its nature. Graphic effects have been applied to some of the images to further reveal and unlock their nature for visual acuity. The original intention is un-retouched and unprocessed process.

The poetry was inspired by the images muttering in my consciousness. The ideas are expressed in free verse and stream of consciousness. Each image whispers a story in poetic memes. **Masks & Mirrors** may reveal to observers clues to their own consciousness.

The graphic and poetic depictions may not inspire, but may cause one to inquire. Allow your inner inquiry to ignite into the flame that is your being.

Take off your Mask and look into the Mirror.

ACKNOWLEDGMENTS

This book of art and poetry is an offering to Spirit in gratitude for my breath, and abundance of blessings that have been bestowed upon my life.

My wife, Debra Podjed, has been a profound inspiration of love and creativity in my life.

Dogo Barry Graham, a wonderful friend and inspiration, encouraged me to publish.

Melanie Pahlmann and Bill Georgevitch have supported and encouraged me in my creativity.

Robin Reiss offered her insight and encouragement into my artistic inquiry.

Masks & Mirrors

vision, perception, deception, affection, conception

shifting spheres of reality that change with

light and shadow, today and tomorrow

illuminating, ruminating, undulating and associating

looks like, feels like, could be, should be, may be?

themes and variations, incarnations and reincarnations

incantations and celebrations

cerebral, ceremonial, fictional, fanciful and functional

in-exacting extracting, sometimes distracting

play acting

seeing without looking, allowing and flowing

non-attachment to outcomes and out-goes

words and pictures

renderings and writings

exploration

Seeing is Being

Masks & Mirrors Too

journey to the archaic arcane

magic and mystery

shamans, demons, angels and familiars all lie here

sometimes raw, atavistic, juvenile — genuine and fake

sometimes jaundiced, joking and distorted

masks reveal more than they hide

identity is both fractured and featured

put on your mask or try one of mine

when the play is over they all come off backstage

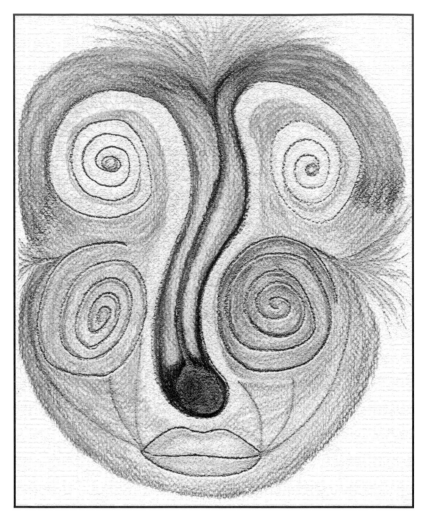

Whimsy Who

Whimsy Who

who are you?

you are a curious creature of spiral definition

you appear impossible and inane to clouded minds

you are unique, one of a kind

without homogenous humor

you are the clown, the jester

pointing out the pointless

mocking accepted norms and conventions

revealing truth

shrouded in your laughter and cunning wit

draw me into your spiral depths

that I may get the cosmic joke

and laugh with you unrestrained

Altar-ed State

Altar-ed State

altar-ed state in blissful being
found in Samadhi

eyes see, yet no longer search
no higher realm or dimension to attain

perception altar-ed and restored
let me imbibe freely from your well
so that I may no longer thirst

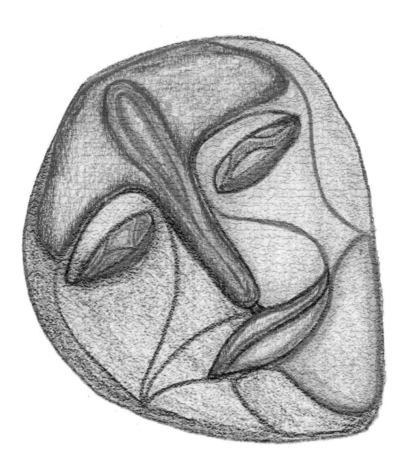

Angel

Angel

being of smiling supernal bliss

sublime countenance of kindness

always present in my life

shining joy in the darkness

gratitude fills my heart,

as I look into the mirror of your love

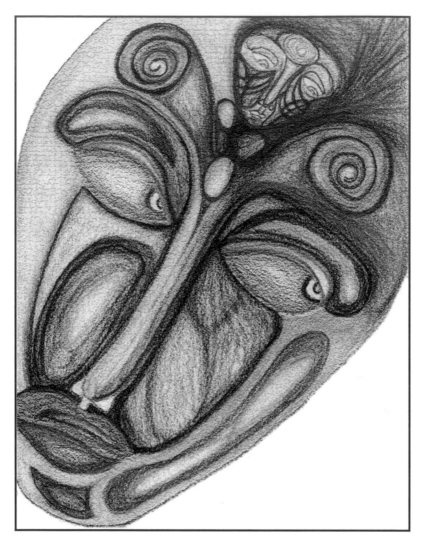

Avatar

Avatar

mind within mind

eternal spirals of light and being

line your enchanted countenance

your being enfolds me in mystic contemplation

I bow to your wisdom

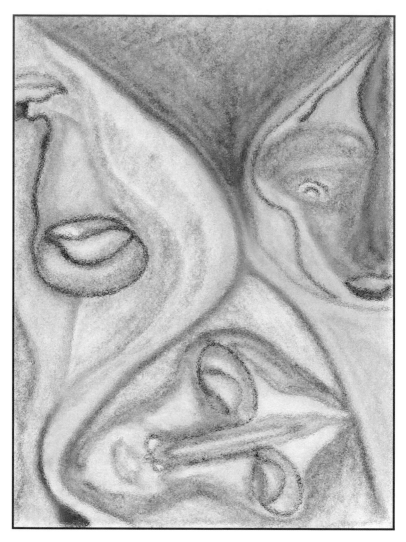

Cosmic Faces Underwater

Cosmic Faces Underwater

mirrors of ecstatic being

turn your face toward me

that your beauty might merge with mine

I see your ancient currents

that map the universal flow

of selfless soul travel in all worlds

your liquid light unites dimensions

and gathers consciousness

as your faces merge into being

Cosmic Stream

Cosmic Stream

beings of infinite grace

filling the worlds with your wisdom

you move through cosmic currents

dispensing your generative force

immerse me into your celestial flow

that I may merge into you!

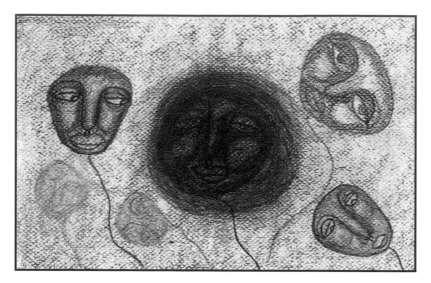

Floating

Floating

beings floating silently

slowly rising to unknown heights

floating faces finding their way in unchartered sky

not attached to earth or destination

trusting spirit to inspire

Genii

Genii

your face engraved with ancient spirals

clear thought issues from crystal white luminance

dreams and dreamer combine

molding eternity

let me gaze through your vision

to become the genii that is me

Hochmah Allatu

Hochmah Allatu

oh ancient goddess of ageless wisdom

the light of your sun shines through the maya

your hair of rainbow light streams down upon the earth

bring sacred harmony here, now

to a humanity that is trapped in the morass

of its own making

we welcome your love and guidance

Moon and Sun

Moon and Sun

draped in darkness

freely giving and reflecting your radiance

your lips contain galaxies of sage light

peering out from the void

into crystal suspended stillness

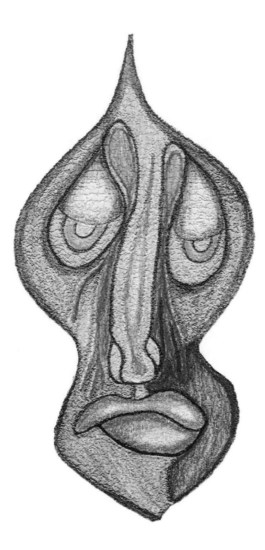

Perplexed

Perplexed

perplexed, entranced and confounded

mysteries hidden in plain sight

the mind that feels senses the subtleties of being

turn your eyes to the inner plane

the place where eternity plays

allow your thoughts to be transformed

by compassion and loving kindness

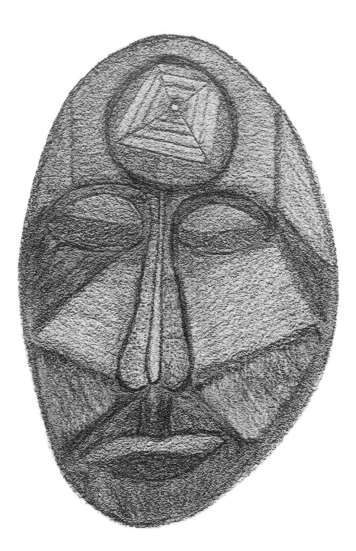

Pyramidal Fusion

Pyramidal Fusion

merging metals
revealing dimensional states
your third eye transfixed
from the ancient temple mound

gold silver and bronze
mined in deep space,
line your visage and bring to earth
your primordial world

as I gaze into your pyramidal eye
my sight returns to origins of light
as your precious metals
shield me from illusion

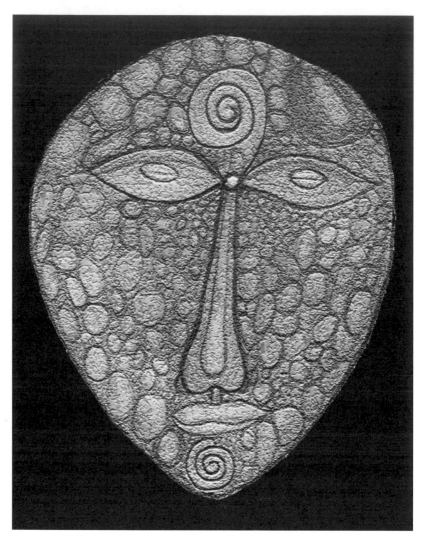

Reptilian Too on Stone

Reptilian Too on Stone

forgotten artisans

carved your image in stone face

tribal totem of immeasurable import

to all who follow the coiled path of being

your spiral third eye draws me deep

into unchartered dimensions of arcane wisdom

I am awed by your ancient visage

Tree Spirit

Tree Spirit

spirit of the tree

looking intently upon the earth

all find succor in the shade of your glance

strength and grace are your portion and offerings

always present divine sylvan mother

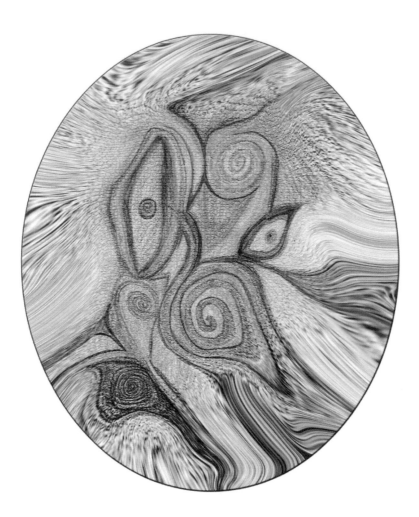

Warrior Monk

Warrior Monk

warrior monk of ancient order

your fierce glance shatters illusion

liquid luminance flows through your countenance

as my battles rage

your gaze pierces my ancient crafted armor

I am left dead on the battlefield

where I am finally released from ego

Fluid Faces Darkened

Fluid Faces Darkened

fluid faces darkened meaning

your countenances obscured by tainted introspection

the observer casts the shadow of narcissistic dreams

attached to deluded desires

show me your true face

let me see you as I am

that I transform into fluid reality

Big Eyes

Big Eyes

big eyes peering through cosmic gas

light reflections beaming back from ancient stars

whose eyes are these looking into me?

can being so immense see me, a speck of dust?

you follow me whether I turn or stay

I feel rays of life infuse my soul

watch over me that I may see through you

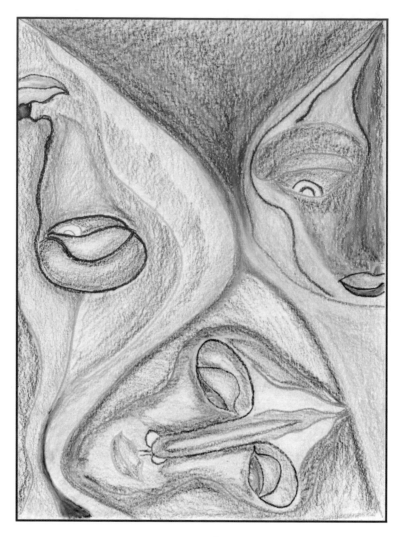

Cosmic Faces

Cosmic Faces

mirrors of ecstatic being

turn your face toward me

that your beauty might merge with mine

I see your ancient lines

that map the universal flow

of selfless soul travel

in all worlds your ribbon light

unites dimensions and gathers consciousness

as your faces merge into being

Dazed and Confused

Dazed and Confused

spiral vortexes of imagined meaning

grinning teeth barred and naked

exposed to reveal narcissistic illusions

you show me the self-centered dream

and reveal the suffering grimace

of self-centered thoughts

I see the illusion, the façade of self

in your mesmerizing eyes

I see through you and me

and find compassion

Elementals

Elementals

earth, air, fire and water

being that permeates all life

I cry out to you in desperate times

humans have forgotten the binding forces

the intimate union of life

forgive our arrogance, our vanity

our human-centric blindness

that separates us from being

Fluid Faces

Fluid Faces

fluid faces flowing through dimensional windows

undulating visages of sinuous suppleness

your mercurial formless forms mutate and undulate

outside of gravitational influences

unaffected by normal space

you exist in planes of conscious fluidity

not bound by temporal or spatial vectors

no affairs of causality or personality

free from dualistic consternation

your free form flows in the cosmic stream

you transport me in fluidic mind

to a place of bliss without origin or reference

I slipstream through your pure consciousness

infuse me with fluidic being

that the faces of the cosmos may radiate through me

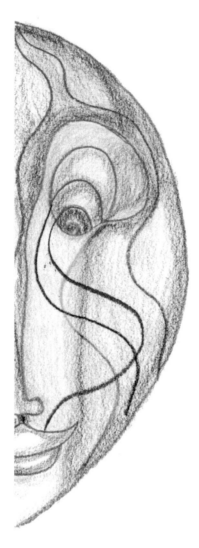

Happy Half

Happy Half

happy half
joyful side of life

let the streams of ribbon joy
that line your face
flow into darkened places

too much bliss to reveal your full countenance
smile through my heart
that all may feel your light

Moon Rising

Moon Rising

moon rising in sun's wake

your mysterious light

illuminates darkened earthscapes

fiery mountain silhouettes

emblazoned on your beautiful face

glowing molten crags of ancient earth and stone

cool in your tranquil presence

searing earth calms

as it surrenders to water's passion

caressed in its earthen bowl

night erupts in phosphorescent luminance

as you tend the naked wounds of scorching day

enfold me in your light

that I may heal in your cooling

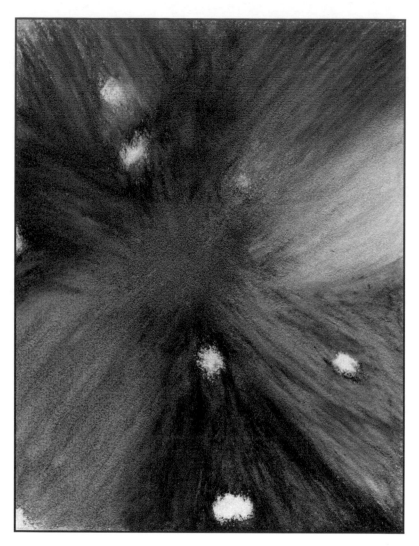

Nebula

Nebula

floating in infinite expanse

gaseous clouds of stardust

reflecting myriad spectrums of rainbow luminance

portals of light allow entrance into your inner being

dark and light majestic radiance

you rule over space-time

infinite stars and planets are birthed in your womb

star children dance in sparkling wonder

I rejoice in your splendor

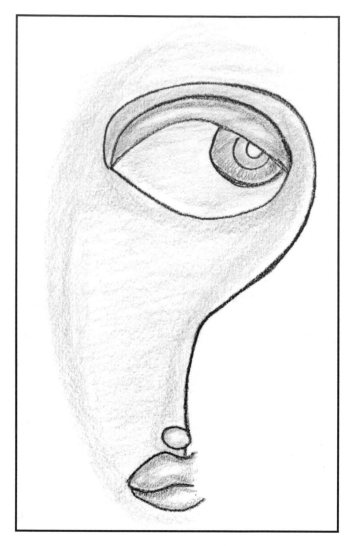

Question Marked

Question Marked

eye-mage

looking into mysterious mysts

half in this world and half in that

where will you look next?

is the truth, the truth?

or just another dead end?

the truth you don't see now

is on the side that has faded from this world

believe not in what you see with the world eye

look through the unseen eye and see

Questions

Questions

looking out from curious minds the questions never end

the answers that bring no succor

the asking is from fear

the asking is from an age old illness

the clarity that comes from stillness

dispels clouded truth

the mind just wanders here

look above and look below

the eyes will tell you where

look without and look within

you are already there

ABOUT THE AUTHOR

John P. Hinton, aka Muttering Madzub, is a contemplative poet, writer, blogger, artist, musician and gardener.

A student of compassionate Being, learning to live in the moment …writing, drawing, singing, and speaking — uncensored, irreverent, unconventional and unrefined.

John pushes the envelope of accepted thought and dogma with an invitation to take off the mask and look into the mirror. He's been known to throw in a bit of religion, politics and social commentary as well.

This Muttering Madzub questions safe havens of belief — ideas of self, god, and the universe.

Phoenix, Arizona is home where John lives on Karma Farma with his wife Debra, Karma Kitty, fish and feral felines.

Made in the USA
Charleston, SC
30 January 2013